IT'S ALL GREEK TO ME

CONFESSIONS OF AN UNLIKELY ACADEMIC

DAVID ALAN BLACK

Energion Publications
Gonzalez, FL
2014

Cover Photo:
ID 3716867 © Jarvis Gray | Dreamstime.com

ISBN10: 1-63199-039-X
ISBN13: 978-1-63199-039-7

Energion Publications
P. O. Box 841
Gonzalez, FL 32560

http://energion.com
pubs@energion.com
850-525-3916

Dedicated to all the hypocrites and fools like me.
May God help us to find the Way.

ACKNOWLEDGMENTS

To begin with, it is my great pleasure to offer special thanks to my publisher, Henry Neufeld. With his usual aplomb and enthusiasm, he bravely accepted this strand of mental floss for publication. I am especially grateful for his partnership in the Gospel, a partnership that only close friends can experience to its deepest. I also want to thank my personal assistant, Jacob Cerone – an outstanding young scholar who is always a close and perceptive reader. Lastly, and most importantly, I wish to thank the most important person in my life, who regularly keeps me grounded in the things that truly matter in life. "To Him be glory in the church and in Christ Jesus to all generations, forever and ever. Amen" (Eph. 3:31).

David Alan Black
Rosewood Farm, Virginia

It's All Greek to Me

Over the past 38 years, I have often been asked the question, "Why do you teach Greek?" This is the story of that journey.

Let me begin with the obvious. God has a plan for individuals. And He has communicated this plan to us in His Word. Our God is a communicative God, and He has made known His will to and through His spokesmen who penned the Scriptures. Biblical truth is just that: truth that is communicated in and through the Bible. It is truth that is "inspired by God" and "profitable for teaching, for reproof, for correction, and for training in righteousness, so that the man [or woman] of God may be complete, equipped for every good work" (2 Tim. 3:16).

It is clear that biblical truth is not given for knowledge's sake alone. I therefore emphatically agree with the old Scottish proverb that says, "Greek, Hebrew, and Latin all have their proper place. But it is not at the head of the cross, where Pilate put them, but at the foot of the cross in humble service to Jesus." The ultimate reason for teaching and learning New Testament Greek is that, properly applied, it can issue in a "readiness for every good work" (2 Tim. 2:21)—that is, a life that is equipped to do God's will and go God's way.

What all this implies is that if we are to move from the classroom to real life we will have to prize what we learn and view it as a life skill and not merely as an educational attainment. Of course, this is not easy. Almost all of us feel tremendous ambivalence as we wrestle with the question of just how to apply what we learn in the classroom to the real world. Obviously, knowledge of Greek is essential if we are to have a firm foundation upon which to build our exegesis of the New Testament. On the other hand, I must say forcefully that facts, no matter how brilliantly taught or diligently acquired, are nothing more than the raw building blocks of life.

How we put them together, and for what use (and whose glory), is another matter altogether.

In class, all of us, myself included, have but one Teacher. Together, we look to Him and Him alone for the help we will need both to excel in class and to excel for His glory.

My academic journey could not have been written without Him. The reason is not so much because of all of the time I have spent in the classroom as a student and a teacher. Instead, the reason is because of how that one Teacher has used these years in my life. Behind each year is a host of individuals, ministry opportunities, turning points, trials, investments, sweat, tears, and joy. It is my hope and desire that this peek into some of the milestones of my personal academic journey will be an encouragement to you, wherever you are in your own journey. I have no idea how the Lord might use this, but I am entrusting it to Him and hoping it will be a blessing.

MY LEARNING JUICES START FLOWING

Where and when does an academic journey really begin? I was born on June 9, 1952 in Honolulu, Hawaii. Of course, my journey started there. But my academic journey really began a few years later. Whenever I think about this journey, I think of certain people who were influential and very special to me. For example, at the age of eight a man named Rudy Ulrich arrived in Hawaii. In the late 1950s he planted First Baptist Church Windward. It was he who led me to the Lord when I was eight years of age. Eventually he returned to the mainland and we lost contact, but I have never forgotten him. I will make a beeline for him when I get to heaven. I also thank God for my fifth grade teacher at Kainalu Elementary School. One day she began class with the strange words "¿Cómo está Usted?" It was my first introduction to a foreign language (other than Hawaiian Pidgin). I knew then and there that language learning would be fun and interesting. You could say the seed was planted. I am also grateful for my Kailua High School civics teacher, Mrs. Saranchuk. She helped me look at the world through fresh and insightful eyes. I look back with appreciation for the way she allowed me and a couple of friends to produce a creative slideshow about current issues in Hawaii and present it to the entire student body. She really got my learning juices flowing, and they haven't stopped since.

SURFING TO CHURCH

God still had a lot to do in this young man's heart before heading off to Bible school. Remember that single purpose I mentioned above? On the beaches of Hawaii, the Lord was already preparing me "for every good work" (2 Tim. 2:21). Prior to turning sixteen, I can remember paddling in from the surf to "attend church" on Sunday morning before paddling right back out again to hit the waves. I used to attend a worship service in front of the Hilton Hawaiian Village Hotel sponsored by the Waikiki Beach Chaplaincy (a popular para-church organization at the time). "What happened to First Baptist Church Windward?" you ask. Nothing. I had become involved with the Jesus Movement. This movement was marked by our utter rejection of the institutionalized church, which we all knew was filled with nothing but hypocrites of the worst kind. But for all its strengths (which included going to church on a surfboard), for all its proper emphasis on Jesus, the Jesus Movement was eccentric and off-kilter. And so was I. It wasn't until I was about sixteen that I realized I was just as much a hypocrite as anyone else at First Baptist Church Windward. It was a life-changing lesson. When I plugged back in at FBC Windward, I did much more than was required of me. I led the youth choir, became a deacon, and began serving and not just mooching.

From Biola Student to Biola Instructor

When I finally went to the mainland for college, it was to Biola University in California. Half the advantage of going away to school is, well, going away to school. You're off on your own, making your own way in the world. For me, arriving at Biola in 1971 meant migrating from the balmy climes of Hawaii to the invigorating intellectual atmosphere of Southern California. I was doing, literally, what no one in my family had done before. I had gone to college. I became captivated in school by the biblical languages, the wisdom of the church fathers, the skepticism of the skeptics, and the theology of the theologians. My Greek professor in college, Dr. Sturz, did his best to weed me out, but little did he know that I was destined (divine passive!) to be a lifelong student of New Testament Greek. Though I had to drop his beginning Greek class, I was able to complete my first year of Greek studies through Moody Bible Institute's correspondence course. Eventually Dr. Sturz hired me to teach eleven units of Greek at Biola, which meant that I could indulge in my favorite pastime and get paid for it.

Boy Meets Girl

At Biola I met many people who were influential in my academic journey. One of them was more influential than any other in my life. We actually met in the cafeteria line at the university. I remember offering her a chocolate-covered macadamia nut, and the rest (as they say) is history. I graduated from Biola in 1975, and in 1976 I married a beautiful Southern lady, Becky Lapsley, in her home church in Dallas, Texas. When we met, Becky was studying nursing and I was a Biblical Studies major. Marriage was not an easy decision for me. I had come from a broken home, and I knew that God's original blueprint for marriage was seldom followed or modeled, even in Christian homes. The picture is one of total unselfishness, two persons actively and joyfully fulfilling their duties to their partners. It involves mutual love and respect, a unity

4

of purpose and goals. Is anyone ever ready for that step? Ready or not, we said our "I do's" on September 11, 1976, in a beautiful ceremony at Grace Bible Church, where Dwight Pentecost was pastoring. Becky was glowing in her lovely traditional wedding gown, while I wore a simple white shirt and trousers with a maile lei—the usual wedding garb for a man in Hawaii. Needless to say, a few eyebrows were raised in tradition-loving Dallas. Though Dr. Pentecost participated in the service, our pastor from California, Robert Hakes of the College Church, performed the ceremony.

Marriage, as Peter Marshall once said, is not a federation of two sovereign states. It is a union of lives, the confluence of two tributaries that, after being joined together in marriage, flow together in the same channel, sharing the same joys and carrying the same burdens. This is the wonderful goal of a Christian marriage, but it comes at a high price. When two strong, independent people flow together, a lot of power is generated. The current can be very strong and difficult to handle. Rare is the husband who can come into a marriage understanding his wife's needs. He tends to think his job is to provide a living instead of sharing a life. He lacks the tenderness and care that a deeply satisfying relationship requires. In our marriage Becky and I had to continually adjust, continually adapt, continually grow. But God honored our commitment to each other. If I talk about my marriage it's not because mine was perfect but because it was the only marriage I knew deeply. For 37 years we learned how to survive and thrive, flex and forgive, using the principles of God's Word. Our only claim was God's amazing grace that enabled us to keep on flowing together in an ever-deepening unity of heart and purpose.

THE STURZ IMPRINT

When I was hired to teach Greek at Biola it was a dream come true. I was like a boy taking his first theology lesson and saying that he would like to be a Karl Barth. The salary was microscopic, but in those days very little could be expected if one was a humble instructor. This was during my second year of seminary at Talbot School of Theology. It was the same year that I married Becky. We used Chase and Phillips' classical grammar for beginning Greek. It was designed to be covered in one semester at Harvard, but we scraped by in two. Students were obligated to translate, parse, and endure quizzes and exams. I was closely supervised by the head of the Greek department, Dr. Sturz. No one was kinder to me, or more encouraging. I was bent, grimly and ferociously, on mastering every secret of Chase and Phillips. I must have succeeded, as I was hired again in 1977. I think my chief intellectual adventure in those days was my interaction with Professor Sturz. His noble features showed little trace of the burden of years, and he had already been a legend for years on campus as a symbol of excellent teaching. "He taught as one having authority, and not as the scribes." All of us recognized his immense intellect. Yet he was never dogmatic, never over-bearing. It was there at Biola in the 1970s, under the tutelage of this gentleman scholar, that I honed whatever skills I possess as a Greek teacher. He left his imprint on my life.

Less Is More

It was during this time at Biola that I started thinking about pedagogy. It is said that the best teachers have an intuitive understanding of the learning process. For me, understanding the learning process has not been very intuitive; I've had to enroll in the school of hard knocks. For example, here's one lesson I've had to learn the hard way: Whenever we simply ask our students to fill in their notebooks while we lecture, education tends to be curtailed and genuine learning retarded. This is because of what I call the First Law of Paid-agogy. My pattern of lecturing was the one my teachers at Biola had used. As a student, I called it the "You Sit Still and I Instill" method. That is to say, I was under the impression that my job as a teacher—what I was getting paid to do (hence the title First Law of Paid-agogy)—was to disseminate information. The more information, the better. As the years went by, however, I couldn't help saying to myself, "I wonder just how many of these facts my students will remember after they've graduated?" Then I had an epiphany. "Why not allow the students to get all the hard facts by reading the textbook before coming to class? If I did that, could I perhaps spend class time focusing on more relevant (and intrinsically important) material?" The more I pondered these questions, the more it seemed obvious to me that the principle of "less is more" works in the classroom as much as it does in any other venue of life. To be sure, I still felt it was my duty to see that my students learned the hard facts of the discipline they were studying—New Testament Introduction, for example. My only question was, "Why spend valuable class time lecturing over this material when the students can get it in one fourth the time by reading it in a textbook, especially a well-written one?" This understanding of pedagogy continues to influence the way I teach today, and I believe my students are the better for it.

Missiology, Greek, and Missions

After I graduated from Talbot in 1980, Becky and I had the opportunity to move to Switzerland for my doctoral studies. Here's a bit a trivia which you may not have known about me: I once considered becoming a missiologist. In fact, in 1978 I met with the great German missiologist Peter Beyerhaus in Tübingen, where we discussed the possibility of me doing a Ph.D. under him in the area of missions. My dissertation topic was going to be on the history of Christian missions in the Hawaiian archipelago, a fitting topic for someone who was hatched and raised in the Islands. Dr. Beyerhaus very kindly informed me that he was willing to work with me should I decide to enter Tübingen as a doctoral student.

Today I am becoming the missiologist I have always wanted to be. Not in any professional sense, of course. I have neither the time nor the patience to pursue another doctorate, nor do I feel it's necessary to be credentialed to serve Christ as an educated "layperson." If a cobbler could become a catalyst for missions, why not a student of ancient Greek? And if I should occasionally give up the comforts of the U.S. for the hardships of Alaba or Burji in Ethiopia, this is nothing to boast about: it is the way of the missionary to be willing to do whatever, wherever. A point that Andrew Walls makes in his book *The Missionary Movement in Christian History* is that missiology should not exist for itself. It is impossible, he argues, to separate missiology from the other academic disciplines. The biggest obstacle is institutional: we have compartmentalized and professionalized "missions studies" instead of seeking to cross-fertilize our thinking about missions with the other theological disciplines (thus developing, for example, a missiological Christology, a missiological ecclesiology, etc.). I don't want to give the impression that I am against sub-disciplines such as New Testament, Evangelism, or Church History. The problem, as I see it, is that our colleges, seminaries, and many of our churches have lost sight of where they ought to be heading. Priorities are not set along missionary lines. Our sub-disciplines have therefore taken on a life of their own. It ought to be apparent that missions is central to the biblical revelation. Then why should it be marginalized? The devil cannot stand it when we get rid of our hidden academic pride and prejudice and make a real commitment to doing what God wants us to do with our lives.

Getting Ready for Switzerland

Before we left for Basel in 1980, Becky and I went on a short-term mission trip to West Germany. I'll never forget it. The year was 1978, and we had been married for only two years. Our orientation took place in the hallowed halls of Wheaton College in Illinois, which Greater Europe Mission used for training purposes. Not a single one of us short-termers begrudged our time in Wheaton. The goal of our orientation was three-fold, as I recall: to reduce the stress upon our arrival in Germany, to help us avoid making needless cultural gaffes, and to bind us together as a team. My own team of missionaries (I played trumpet on a brass octet that did evangelism) needed to be reminded that shoddiness was unacceptable. Hence we practiced and practiced until we could play our music almost flawlessly. Some of us who could speak German also practiced our testimonies with each other. I memorized mine. It began, "Hat die Musik Ihnen gut gefallen?" That line was, hopefully, the entrée into a discussion about Jesus and the Gospel. The team's tuba player and I eventually developed a very close friendship. Our team also discussed the do's and don'ts of German society. This experience taught me to not overlook thorough preparation when it comes to missions. The most important preparation is spiritual.

LIFE IN BASEL

When we finally arrived in Basel, Becky and I lived in a one-room apartment. To be more exact, we lived in the Parterre, which was about as low as you could get (both spatially and in terms of societal status). You might say that our life was primitive enough to have satisfied Rousseau. We were not permitted to shower or bathe after 10:00 pm per city ordinance. Nor could we control our own heat. The landlord controlled the heat for the whole building. We often had to take hot baths to stay warm during the winter. We had a tiny bathroom and an even smaller kitchenette. But happiness does not depend on physical furnishings. We had youth and vigor. Most of all we had the Lord. Life was very simple. I toiled over my dissertation while Becky kept busy with her hobbies, including practicing the piano. On occasion, we entertained. One day Becky worked feverishly to prepare our table for the arrival of some much esteemed dinner guests—none other than Professor and Mrs. Reicke. The latter was a bit taken aback when she entered our humble abode. After all, most of her husband's students hailed from Princeton and Harvard, not from a nondescript seminary called Talbot. Our low "social status" had no effect on the way my esteemed professor treated me. Professor Reicke was extremely kind. He gave me access to his personal library, and we enjoyed many pleasant conversations together—something perhaps unusual in a day and age when a student's chair was not supposed to be cushioned with any intimacy. I took far too little recreation in that era. Still, we did a good bit of walking, despite the ease with which we could have traveled "mit 'em Dram" (with the tram).

Typically speaking, in the United States students meet with their professors on campus. Not so in Switzerland. Neither my major professor nor any other professor at the university had an office on campus. So if one wanted to discuss anything with them, one had to meet with them in their homes. I was frequently a guest of Bo and Ingelisa Reicke and an occasional visitor at the home of Oscar Cullmann on the famous Birmannsgasse. One time I had the privilege of sharing a meal with Professor Markus Barth and his wife at their villa in Riehen, just outside Basel on the German border. Naturally I discovered many reasons for preferring Basel above the UK universities. It scarcely occurred to us Doktoranden that we should go anywhere else.

THE LECTURE HALL IN BASEL

When I matriculated at the University of Basel, I registered for seven courses. In those days we did not have to attend lectures unless we wanted to. Your professor simply signed your Testatbuch at the beginning of the semester and again at the end. For all he knew, you might actually be taking a course at a different university. The system worked well—if you were a self-starter. Basically, it was the honor system, which I use today in my classes (I never take attendance). I studiously attended every lecture. I will never forget my first classroom experience. As Jan Milic Lochman entered the lecture hall, we students ceased our chattering and rapped our knuckles in applause. For sixty minutes Professor Lochman poured forth a torrential stream of eloquence about his hero Comenius, that great Czech theologian. As the hour struck, he stopped and walked out amid a tumult of cheering. And so it was with most of my lectures. Occasionally a visiting lecturer would offer public lectures in Basel, and in 1980 this included none other than Francis Schaeffer. As a fellow American I cheered him vociferously, but most of his audience was lukewarm at best, probably because the good doctor was highly critical of Swiss society at the time. A handful of other Americans were attending the university at the time (the names David Moessner and Donald Verseput come to mind). I recall standing out as the only alkoholfrei American in the group, nor did I smoke a pipe, as did so many of the other doctoral students. (Markus Barth's seminars were filled with so much pipe smoke that I am certain I will succumb to lung cancer one day as a result.) I once accepted an invitation to attend Bernard Wyss's course on reading ninth century Greek minuscule manuscripts, the reward for which was a visit to the sub-basement of the University Library, where an original 1516 edition of the Erasmus Greek New Testament was physically placed in my hands—a rare volume that I greatly desired to steal, as improper as such an act would have been for a Basel Doktorand.

"What about exams?" you ask. There were no exams at all, save the orals at the end of my program and the inaugural Greek and Latin orals. The theory was, of course, that doctoral students were highly self-motivated and loved to work independently of extrinsic motivations. I wish that as an undergraduate I could have experienced this kind of freedom, but in college we were treated like glorified high school students. At any rate, I still possess the love of learning that I mastered while a student in Basel, and I got some inkling of what the Germans meant by that mysterious word *Innigkeit*. Eventually I graduated with high honors and life returned to normal, but the radiant happiness and excitement of those old days along the Rhine have never left me.

I was often invited to coffee mostly by Germans or South Koreans to discuss theology in one of the local Stuben. As perhaps the only inerrantist among the Doktoranden, I was assaulted mercilessly, but I managed to stand my ground, and no friendships were broken over our disagreements. (I never did become a Barthian.) When I was not in class, I was researching my dissertation topic in the University Library, which, as you may know, allows no access to the shelves. It often took an hour or more for an attendant to find a book. As a matter of fact, the Theologisches Seminar had its own theological library to which we doctoral students were granted unlimited access night and day, and it was there that one could usually find me during the afternoon and evening hours.

The winter of 1980 in Basel was the coldest I have ever experienced. Even the Swiss were commenting on how frigid the temperatures were that year. But our social life suffered little as a result. Once a month Becky and I would take in a free organ concert at one of the city's cathedrals, and every Friday evening we treated ourselves to the one and only MacDonald's restaurant in town. Becky would order a Big Mac, while I insisted on my Filet-O-Fish. Once we attended a symphony orchestra concert where we happened to run into the Reickes. Because of our close association with the Baptist community in the city (we had joined die Baptistengemeinde Basel), we were frequently invited to eat with one of the church families, either in their home or in a local restaurant. A very good time was had by all, I do believe. Friendships such as these made our stay in that city on the Rhine a richly rewarding one.

Becky and I found Basel a fascinating city. The ancient buildings and narrow streets had scarcely been altered since the days of Erasmus and Calvin. The Great Minster afforded a spectacular view of the Rhine, while the ruins of Kaiser Augst ("Caesar Augustus") took one back in time to the Roman occupation of "Basilea" some

2,000 years ago. Sometimes we dined in a restaurant overlooking the Middle Rhine Bridge (a local landmark) and watched the barges on their way down the river to Rotterdam. I frequently patronized the local bookshops, even though I had no money to buy anything. On Sunday mornings we faithfully attended the Gottesdienst, where there were never more than thirty or forty people in attendance. If I recall correctly, I preached four or five times there (in High German) before we returned to the States.

Sometimes Becky and I would tramp together in the Black Forest or the Vosges, and I clearly remember one day standing on the exact spot in the middle of the Rhine where Germany, France, and Switzerland meet. We also managed a trip to Greece during this time, where, believe it or not, I fell in love with okra, a vegetable I had previously detested.

MEETING MY DOKTORVATER

I remember my first meeting in Basel with Bo Reicke. The prodigal son couldn't have had a warmer welcome. I can still remember how he shook my hand and said how glad he was that I had come to Basel. I knew immediately that I was glad too. My experience was amazing. Of course, that was all the Lord's doing. He knew I would benefit from studying under Bo Reicke. A kinder man never graced any university campus. No one could know the man without having his or her life touched permanently. I will be forever grateful to God for that wonderful experience.

One seminar I took with Professor Reicke entailed translating the Greek and Latin Fathers. We were asked to come to class each week prepared to recite and translate without any notes whatsoever. After two semesters of these grammatical drills we were expected to sit for our Greek and Latin orals that were personally administered by our Doktorvater. Since I had already been teaching classical Greek at Biola, I fared well in the seminar, though Latin was a bit of a challenge as I had merely taught myself the language out of a textbook. I enjoyed everything Professor Reicke did in his classes, but in this seminar his wit and humor seemed to evaporate. Only grammar and dull recitation remained. I obeyed strictly the rules forbidding the use of translations, though more often than not "I found out the Latin by the meaning rather than the meaning by the Latin" (to paraphrase Samuel Johnson). At any rate, Professor Reicke evidently felt it his duty to examine me after only one semester, and I received a passing grade in both languages. I disliked the drudgery of rote translation intensely, but today I chalk that up to boyish folly. Since then I have been associated with grammars my entire academic career, and have toiled hard over the grammar of many languages. The irony is that I am absurdly ignorant of the formal rules of English grammar and often have to rely on the English majors in my classes to resolve points of controversy.

PASSING THROUGH THE LINGUISTIC FIRES

As a student in Basel I was expected to speak German fluently, unless incapacitated by sheer terror, or by immovable obstinacy. How then did I learn the language? Quite simply: from a book. That is, from several conversational German grammars. (They're all basically the same, of course, but variety is the spice of life, right?) But how did I learn to speak the language? Ah, that's another story altogether, and the answer is: Mr. Paul Mittmann. Herr Mittmann had emigrated to Anaheim, California after World War II, as did so many others from Germany after the war. He got a job and also pastored a small Lutheran Brethren congregation there, and since it met early on Sunday morning I could attend its German-speaking service before going to my home church in La Mirada. Eventually we began to meet together weekly for grammar and pronunciation lessons.

Like the language he was teaching, Herr Mittmann was hard, clear, and sharp as a winter dawn. Hailing from East Prussia, he spoke impeccable Ost-Preussen, considered by many Germanophiles to be the purest form of the language. Paul Mittmann was neither talkative nor taciturn, neither sanguine nor phlegmatic, neither excitable nor lugubrious. He kept an even course and held just the right temper in his relationships with everybody. Without arrogance, he exuded confidence and had a remarkable talent for sorting out complicated issues by cutting through them with a swathe of quiet logic. We discussed many topics together in German, from theology to his wartime experiences. He had been inducted into the Wehrmacht when he was 18 and had seen action on almost every front, from Poland to Italy to France. After the war he and his wife lived under an overturned military vehicle for a year in the western part of Germany, along with hundreds of thousands of others of DPs (displaced persons) who had fled from the east in 1945. How he became the pastor of a German-speaking congregation in America, I am not sure; but he was an excellent speaker and a wonderfully caring personality.

Once, after I had been attending the church for several weeks, he turned to me and asked, "Would you like to read the Scripture next week?" That really put me on the spot, but as I was blown away by the special emphasis he had given to the public reading of Scripture I found myself the next Sunday reading from the Luther-Bibel during the Gottesdienst. Not long afterward he had me preaching in German during his absence, much to the delight of the aging congregation who, I feel, were happy to have a young person in their midst and thus were willing to overlook the blunders of a fledgling speaker.

And so there was Herr Mittmann, undeniably, indisputably German, and above all else a fellow believer in Christ, to my astonishment taking me under his wings as a master would his apprentice. I have often wondered what my experience in German-speaking Basel would have been like had it not been for his willingness to help out an American student whose father had been wounded in 1945 while fighting Germans. There is no question in my mind who profited more from this relationship, and I shall forever be in his debt.

The real difficulty in my acquisition of the German language arose in Basel. I had not been informed that the Swiss have their own particular dialect of German. I had no practice in Swiss German and was terrified of it. Fortunately, I managed to find a Basel German grammar in a local bookstore. All at once, things began to fall into place. The vowels were easy enough, but the consonantal shifts were perplexing. I soon found myself guessing, and of course I guessed wrong. Back to the grammar, I told myself. One could not help but be aware that learning Basel German made High German look like child's play. I formed the habit of speaking dialect whenever the opportunity arose, though I was overwhelmed at first by the pressure it put on my tired brain. My French was even more problematic. On outings into the Vosges I tried my best to speak the language, but I took some pretty hard knocks. Was I a philologist, and could I ever become one? My French interlocutors, I'm afraid, would have answered that question in the negative. On visits to the Reickes I would sometimes hear them speaking on the phone. The conversation often took place in Swedish (their mother tongue) but just as often in English, French, German, or even Italian. I imagine they felt sorry for me because I was so linguistically challenged. As I said before, on Sunday mornings we would attend the German-speaking Baptist church in Basel, and I preached there on several occasions. I know no one who did not sincerely appreciate my efforts at communicating in German. My accent left something to be desired, however. In Switzerland I was often mistaken for a German, and in Germany for a Swiss. As a result I began to work very hard on my enunciation and, for the most part, have succeeded in passing myself off for a German in Germany—which still surprises me.

Blessings in Basel

I can hardly fail to mention how grateful I am for our friends in Basel who took us under their wings while we were "sojourners and exiles" in a foreign land. I think, for example, of Frau Schaub of our church there, who tutored Becky weekly in German. As a result, within three months Becky was speaking the language. What a sacrifice of love! Perhaps this is why Becky and I had so much room in our heart for international students. While in Switzerland I had the great honor of meeting Professor Oscar Cullmann. Although he was retired by the time I arrived in Basel in 1980, I was privileged to meet privately with him several times in his home in the Birmannsgasse. He was known in Basel for his outstanding theological exegesis of Scripture. Indeed, I still think his *Christology of the New Testament* is the best book ever written on the subject. Blessings like these are divinely orchestrated parts of our academic journey.

Putting Pen to Paper

I was never trained in the science of linguistics. To tell the truth, I had no interest at all in the subject until I began my doctoral studies. I spent long hours, like graduate students today, in discussing Greek pedagogy with my peers. But I was more interested in pursuing my dissertation topic, which involved biblical theology. I wanted just then to grapple with ideas rather than more grammar. Though I knew that a "D. Theol." was a pleasant ornament to one's name in a college catalog, I desired other things much more. There was at this time, however, no diminution of my love for languages. I was spending long hours reading Greek, Latin, French, and, of course, German. What is more, I began reading what linguists were saying about language, and about how it works, and then applying this knowledge to my exegesis of texts. I was interested in allowing the author to be his own interpreter as much as possible. Thus it was that I began writing my book on linguistics, hoping fervently that someone more qualified would do the job instead.

Upon graduation from Basel in 1983, I revived my courses in Classical and Koine Greek at Biola. I craved for myself as well as for my students a greater mastery of exact terms, and I worked away at my book until Baker agreed to publish it in the late 1980s. *Linguistics for Students of New Testament Greek* was an immediate success, though I fear that linguistics professors objected to my infringement upon their traditional rights. All of us at Biola, I think, gained something from that training in acute observation and accuracy of description that linguistics affords. In the meantime, my essays were being accepted for publication in such journals as *Biblica*, *New Testament Studies*, and *Novum Testamentum*. More books shortly followed. It is pleasant to remember now my first contacts with my editors at Zondervan, Baker, B & H, and Eisenbrauns. These were men who were willing to take a risk with a young buck. I grew very fond of writing, and am still at it today, though my interests have shifted considerably from the day I published my dissertation in 1984.

"Why So Many Greek Books, Dave?"

Recently I was asked why I've written so many books on Greek. The answer is, "I don't know." I certainly never set out to write books on this language. Writing about Greek doesn't mean that one has mastered the subject. It doesn't even mean that one is a successful classroom teacher. The Greek books I've written have all been written by a learner for learners. I well recall when B & H Academic asked me to write a beginning Greek grammar for them. My response was a polite but firm, "No." *That's all we need—another Greek grammar,* I said to myself. But when they asked me to pray about it, I agreed to do so. A week later I consented, and within four months the book was written. I had a similar experience with my intermediate grammar, *It's Still Greek to Me*. When asked by

Baker Books to write it I again demurred. I knew full well that my friend Dan Wallace was at the time writing an intermediate grammar for Zondervan.

When Dan's work was eventually published, my editor at Baker called me and asked me what I thought of it. With tongue slightly in cheek I replied, "It's the best third year grammar I've ever seen." "Well," he said, "Will you write a genuine intermediate grammar for us?" "Yes," I replied, "as long as I can keep it under 250 pages." Greek is a broad subject. No single textbook can claim to "get it right" in every respect. I know mine can't. For better or for worse my books have been written for the average student—Harvard has yet to approach me about using any of my grammars in their classes! They are also written, to a great degree, from a linguistic perspective. However, let it not be supposed that I have done anything other than scratch the surface. It is hoped that through reading my books the next generation of Greek students will produce their own texts that will far exceed mine both in quality and depth. That said, being a Greek student is one of the most rewarding and joyous avocations possible; and my only prayer is that my few books on the subject might make it even more so.

THE INTERMEDIATE STATE

So what happened after my doctoral program? As I said, when I returned from Basel I picked up my teaching mantel again at Biola, though it was not long before I would be wooed away. In Long Beach an effort was underway by Grace Seminary in Indiana to establish a West Coast Campus. My appointment as academic dean at Grace Graduate School (a ministry of the Grace Brethren Church of Long Beach) was to be the first step in making that a reality. Eventually, Grace West opened its doors as the fully accredited extension campus of Grace Seminary in Winona Lake. I was not so keen about the commute this involved from my home in La Mirada, but the opportunity to reach students with a non-traditional schedule was too good to pass up. Our goal was never to compete with what Biola was doing; our courses were targeted at those students who could only attend classes in the evenings or on the weekends. We were working hard to reach out to the ethnic minorities in Southern California, and were seeing some success. How idealistic I was then! I was brought back to earth sharply. Political dissension on the main campus in Indiana led to the closure of Grace West after only three years of operation. It was an intensely difficult time for me. I saw my vision collapse for what I saw as no good reason.

Back to Biola I went, and there I remained until 1998, though I was also moonlighting at other institutions such as Simon Greenleaf University and Golden Gate Seminary's Brea campus. Personally I owe Biola much—and not merely because it offered me my first chance to earn a living. It was there that I cut my teeth as a classroom teacher under the watchful supervision of Dr. Harry Sturz. He watched me, with those glittering eyes, incessantly. In my classes I was left free to do my work in my way. In the evenings I worked steadily at my writing and tried to keep current with the latest scholarship. It seems to me now that in my early thirties I had more intellectual curiosity and energy than I do now, but in those days the world of academia meant more to me than it does today.

LANDING BETWEEN HONOLULU AND BASEL

In 1998 I was called to Southeastern Seminary, then under its new president, Dr. Paige Patterson. I had no great desire to leave the West Coast, but since several eastern institutions were courting me, I decided to write Dr. Patterson and send him my resume. In November of 1997, Becky and I were flown out to Wake Forest for an interview. I must say it was love at first sight. We were made at home in the spacious Lion House and feted night and day by various members of the faculty. There were many interviews, of course. In the one with the president, I was able to ask any question I wanted. I recall inquiring about office protocol. "How many office hours do you require for your faculty each week?" I asked. I will never forget Dr. Patterson's answer. He smiled at me and said, "Dave, around here we have only one rule: We must all appear before the judgment seat of Christ. Act accordingly." I thought to myself, "This is where I'd like to work!"

Perhaps the most attractive feature of Southeastern for me at that time was its fledgling Ph.D. program in Biblical Studies. I knew that if I ever relocated it would be to a place where I could mentor doctoral students. Thus it was that in the summer of 1998 we moved our horses and goats and settled down in the tobacco fields of Granville County, North Carolina. Some of my work at the seminary, like that of every teacher, is of the grindstone variety, but by no means all. One is almost given carte blanche as to courses and hours, and overloads are usually available. I began teaching the Advanced Greek Grammar course as well as a Ph.D. seminar in Greek Linguistics. I have been able to host three major New Testament conferences on campus, a place of keen enjoyment of academic debate. I have found both the physical climate and the spiritual atmosphere of Southeastern to be more than congenial. I still miss the deserts of the American West, but I have found the pace of life here to be relaxing and soothing after the frantic hubbub of Southern California.

GLOBAL MISSIONS: WILL YOU GO?

At the conclusion of my interview with Paige Patterson in 1997, I was asked a most unusual question. "Dave," he said, "if I were to send you to a level-three security nation on a mission trip, and you knew there was a strong possibility that you would not come back alive, would you go?" As you can well imagine, I had never been asked that question in a job interview before. I requested a minute to think about it, and then I replied, "Yes, sir, I believe I would." I can see clearly enough now what Dr. Patterson was trying to do. I had endeavored, it is true, to be involved in missions prior to coming to Southeastern Seminary. Never before, however, had I been asked to risk my life for the sake of the Gospel. The supreme importance of the Great Commission struck me for the first time in my life. Today, many come to me with questions about how to prioritize the Gospel and integrate it into the rest of their lives. I often ask them the same question I was asked by Dr. Patterson.

Today, Danny Akin has maintained and deepened the commitment at Southeastern to the Great Commission. "Every classroom a Great Commission classroom" is our motto. This is one of the biggest reasons I love teaching at SEBTS. No longer do we have to protect our pet doctrine or our departmental turf. We have a greater responsibility. I believe that 2 Cor. 5:14-21 teaches that we are all to be Christ's ambassadors. We have been given the ministry of reconciliation. This means that every activity, every effort, every program, every project is to be evaluated in terms of how it contributes to the ultimate mission of the church and of the seminary—global evangelization. The Great Commission leaves us no option. Jesus makes no apology for demanding obedience in this area. Global missions is to be the task of every individual Christian and every church and every Christian organization. It is the Lord's final charge to us before He ascended to the Father's right hand. Measured against that, can anything else be more important?

In my book *The Jesus Paradigm* I talked about my life-changing encounter with this Jesus who loved lost souls so desperately that He was willing to spend His ministry reaching out to sinners of all kinds. He saw what was of ultimate importance in life. No wonder He could live for others as a selfless servant. This is also, I believe, the acid test of any seminary that claims to honor Christ. Does what we do square with the Great Commission? Or is our institution just another tangent that detracts from the other-centeredness of the Gospel? It is when we realize that we are building the kingdom and not our own little ministries that the great growth really begins in our lives. When we stop focusing on ourselves, we are free to act on the really important questions. Plainly, I did not always view the purpose of graduate theological education in these terms!

MY DESIRE FOR MY STUDENTS

I began teaching Greek at Biola University in 1976. This means that I've sat through over 30 years of graduation exercise as a faculty member. That calculates to some 70 commencements! I've enjoyed every place I've taught, but there's something special about Southeastern. Jesus invites His followers to join Him in basin ministry. This call to an active ministry permeates the campus. We're asked to love, teach, serve, and go. The hallmark of Jesus' earthly ministry was His willingness to forego what was rightfully His. And that is exactly my prayer today for our grads. Like a Space Shuttle about to be launched, our graduates are sitting on the launching pad about to be propelled into space by thousands of pounds of thrust. The analogy breaks down, of course. In Christianity, the way up is down. Only in defeat do we know victory. Only through weakness do we experience strength. Only as we are on our knees can we ever hope to stand. We do not worship this world. We serve a New King and sing a New Song. We pledge allegiance to Him alone. Our only desire is that His kingdom come, His will be done—through us. In this kingdom, even the least is greater than John the Baptist. This includes even those who do not earn academic honors. Even those who have no idea where God wants to use them. Even those without the trappings of "success." In fact, especially those. I want for my students exactly what Jesus wants for them and from them. He is calling His disciples, saying, "You might not have much, but you can give everything you have to the Cause of Causes. Don't just skim off the top of your abundance. Don't store up for yourselves treasures on earth. Strive for the kingdom and God's righteousness. Then you will have everything." Students, if you hear and obey the biblical message, which urges us to place everything we are and everything we have under the reign of Jesus Christ, you will be truly blessed. You will have an academic journey that you will truly never regret.

Conclusion: The Way Up Is Down

I never set out to become a professional Greek teacher. I "slid" into my teaching career, no doubt with more than a touch of foible about me. I suppose my public reputation is one of a Greek scholar, as far as the academic public is concerned. But my main interests do not catch the public eye. When I began to teach the New Testament documents, I was not mature enough to grasp all of their implications. I have no doubt that, like my Doktorvater in Basel, I was drawn to Gospel studies. To me his lectures on New Testament history were intensely stimulating and made a deep impression on me at the time. I had no doubt that Bo Reicke was on the right side of the synoptic problem. I still think so. It is curious, then, that my dissertation dealt with a problem in Pauline lexicography. It was not until the year 2000 or so that I had the courage to publish my views about the historical origins of the Gospels. But interest is not the same as what God intends for the Gospel to do to our lives. I discovered, in reading the Gospels for myself, that a deep and subtle change was taking place in my life. I had the impression of being in the presence of a great man. In school I had been taught about Christianity; the Gospels were teaching me how to be a Christian. It stole my heart to see such a man as Jesus stoop down and wash His disciples' feet, as if it were a matter of supreme importance to Him. It suddenly increased my own sense of hypocrisy. To discover that you are a professor of New Testament and Greek without possessing the self-effacing mind of your Savior—well, that is life changing.

The way up in the kingdom of God is down. I fear my published attempt to recount the dramatic shift that took place in my life—*The Jesus Paradigm*—is not my best work. But it is as good as I knew how to make it. To my disappointment, *Learn to Read*

New Testament Greek outsells *The Jesus Paradigm* a hundredfold. I do not pretend to be able to explain this. There is certainly less attention in Greek classes to costly service for Christ than the rules and exceptions as set down in the grammars. But who can gaze into the pages of the Gospels and not have his or her life turned upside down? It is as if an old lion has turned in his cage to look at you, only that all the bars have magically disappeared. Life, for me, was undeniably barren until I encountered Jesus. Oddly enough, one can be a full time seminarian (on either side of the desk) and not realize this. So, we are back where we began—at the foot of the cross. The question is whether or not you—and your academic goals and accomplishments—have been placed there for the King to use as he sees fit.

Well?

More from Energion Publications

Personal Study

Finding My Way in Christianity	Herold Weiss	$16.99
The Jesus Paradigm	David Alan Black	$17.99
When People Speak for God	Henry Neufeld	$17.99
The Sacred Journey	Chris Surber	$11.99

Christian Living

Faith in the Public Square	Robert D. Cornwall	$16.99
Grief: Finding the Candle of Light	Jody Neufeld	$8.99
Crossing the Street	Robert LaRochelle	$16.99

Bible Study

Learning and Living Scripture	Lentz/Neufeld	$12.99
From Inspiration to Understanding	Edward W. H. Vick	$24.99
Why Four Gospels	David Alan Black	$11.99
Ecclesiastes: A Participatory Study Guide	Russell Meek	$9.99
Ephesians: A Participatory Study Guide	Robert D. Cornwall	$9.99

Theology

The Politics of Witness	Allan R. Bevere	$9.99
Ultimate Allegiance	Robert D. Cornwall	$9.99
The Church Under the Cross	William Powell Tuck	$11.99
The Journey to the Undiscovered Country	William Powell Tuck	$9.99
Eschatology: A Participatory Study Guide	Edward W. H. Vick	$9.99

Ministry

Clergy Table Talk	Kent Ira Groff	$9.99
My Life Story	Becky Lynn Black	$14.99
Unfettered Spirit	Robert D. Cornwall	$14.99
Wind and Whirlwind	David Moffett-Moore	$9.99
Transforming Acts	Bruce Epperly	$14.99

Generous Quantity Discounts Available
Dealer Inquiries Welcome
Energion Publications – P.O. Box 841
Gonzalez, FL 32560
Website: http://energionpubs.com
Phone: (850) 525-3916

www.ingramcontent.com/pod-product-compliance
Lightning Source LLC
Chambersburg PA
CBHW030011040426
42337CB00012BA/739